CLASSIC GUITAR VOLUME 2

This volume presents and explains the triplet, sixteenth notes and dotted eight note rhythms.

Three-eight and six-eight times are introduced.

The keys employed in this volume are D Major, B Minor, F Major, D Minor, A Major, F♯ Minor and E Major.

The Etudes, Solos and Exercises are carefully graduated in difficulty.

Online Audio   www.melbay.com/93208BCDEB

Mel Bay

Contents

1 2 3 4 5 6 7 8 9 0

At this point, the teacher should start furnishing supplementary material as some of the works in this volume may require more time for completion.

We highly recommend the Mel Bay Folios of Classic Guitar Solos.

Take your time. Develop each page to your utmost ability. Musical enjoyment will be yours.

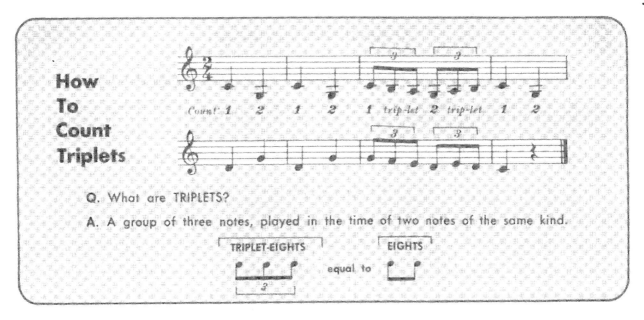

How To Count Triplets

Q. What are TRIPLETS?

A. A group of three notes, played in the time of two notes of the same kind.

TRIPLET-EIGHTS   equal to   EIGHTS

Play the following Triplet Etudes using the following R.H. fingering. pim, pmi, pma, pam.

TRIPLETS

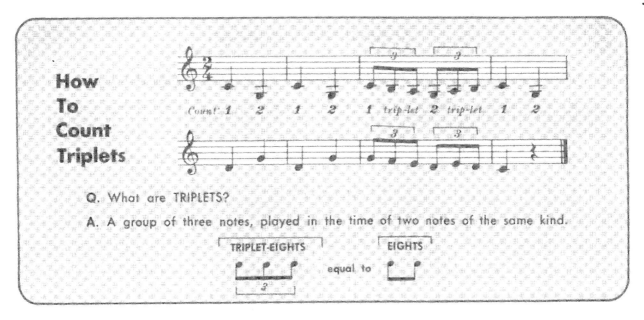

4

Around the Samovar

Right Hand Triplet Etude

REPEAT UNTIL MASTERED

See the "MEL BAY FOLIO OF CLASSIC GUITAR SOLOS"

MODERATO

MAURO GIULIANI

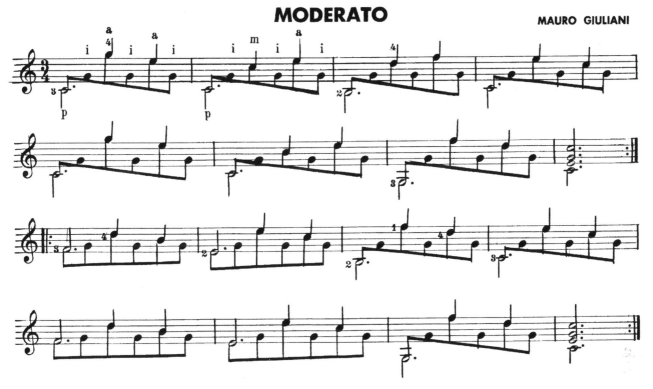

Another Triplet Etude

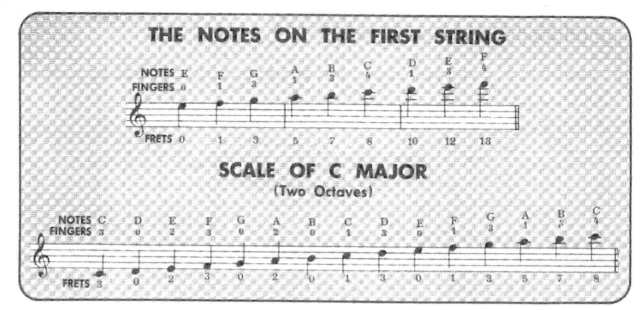

THE SLIDE

The SLIDE is performed by one finger of the left hand sliding over the frets from the first to the second note. The first note is struck and the second note is sounded by the slide.

The slide is indicated by the following sign:

THE SLUR

To execute ascending slurs of two notes, the lower note is to be played and the finger of the left hand descends hammer-like upon the higher note creating the tone desired.

Descending slurs are executed by first fingering the notes to be played with the left hand. Strike the higher note and by drawing the finger sideways off the string, the lower note will automatically sound. Slurred notes will be connected by a curved line. (⌒)

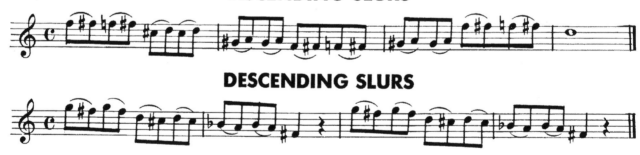

THE SNAP

The SNAP is similiar to the slur in execution. The second note of the SNAP will usually be an open string.

The first note is played and immediately the left hand finger pulls the string sideways as it slides off the fingerboard.

When snapping a note to a closed note, both notes should be held before executing the snap effect.

THE NOTES ON THE SECOND STRING

Shown below are the notes on the second string.

Any note played upon the first string may be played upon the second string **five frets higher** than it's location on the first string.

In the following diagram you will see the notes on the first string and directly below the same notes as played upon the second string. This is a very good aid in remembering the notes on the second string.

THE C SCALE IN THIRDS

The following study should be played upon the first and second strings.

The **top-note will be on the first string** and the **bottom-note on the second.**

To facilitate execution, it is better to let the fingers remain upon the strings as much as possible, gliding from fret to fret.

Carefully observe the fingering.

An Exercise In Thirds

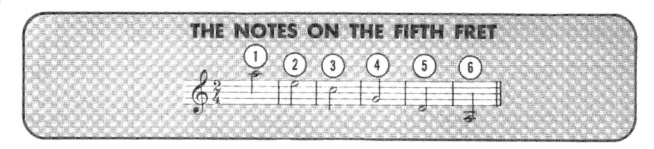

THE NOTES ON THE FIFTH FRET

THE THIRDS IN THE KEY OF G

GUITAR SOLO

Moderato

Granada Memories
(Based upon an etude by Aguado)

MEL BAY

In the above selection employ the R.H. pattern (Pi Pm) throughout except where otherwise shown.

SIXTEENTH-NOTES

In common time four sixteenth-notes equal one quarter-note.

They may be counted in this manner:

1-six-teenth-notes, 2-six-teenth-notes, 3-six-teenth-notes, 4-six-teenth-notes.

Example

TABLE OF NOTES AND RESTS

In the fifth and ninth measures of the following study an eighth note is followed by two sixteenth notes.

They may be counted in this manner:

Sixteenth-Notes

Repeat the above using the following R.H. Fingers: ①pmim, ②pmam, ③pama, ④pima, ⑤pami

Prelude

THREE-EIGHT TIME

This sign 🎼 **3/8** indicates three-eight time.

3 — — beats per measure.

8 — — type of note receiving one beat. (eight note)

An eighth-note ♪ = one beat, a quarter-note ♩ = two beats and a dotted quarter-note

♩. = three beats. A sixteenth-note ♬ = ½ beat.

Petite Waltz

Carcassi's Waltz

THE KEY OF D MAJOR

The Key of D Major will have two sharps—F♯ and C♯.

To facilitate the fingering in the Key of D Major, it is necessary to move the first finger to the second fret, the second finger to the third fret and the third finger to the fourth fret. (Note scale)

THE D MAJOR SCALE

Exercise

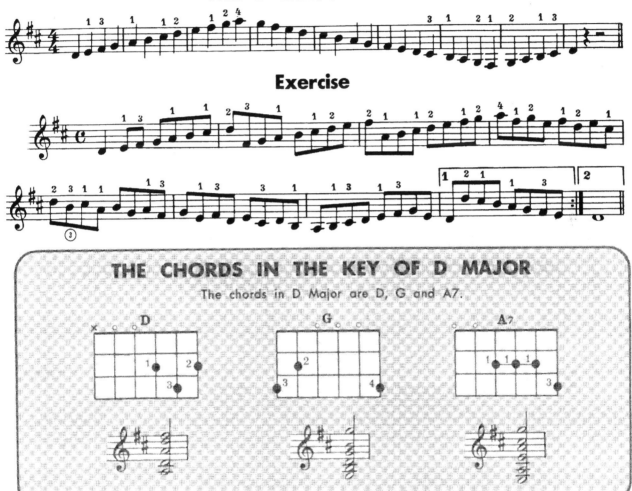

THE CHORDS IN THE KEY OF D MAJOR

The chords in D Major are D, G and A7.

Accompaniment Styles

12

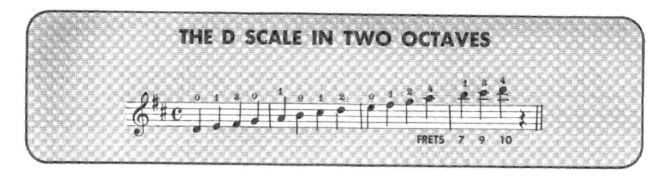

THE D SCALE IN TWO OCTAVES

FRETS 7 9 10

Prelude

Etude

CARCASSI

THIRDS IN THE KEY OF D

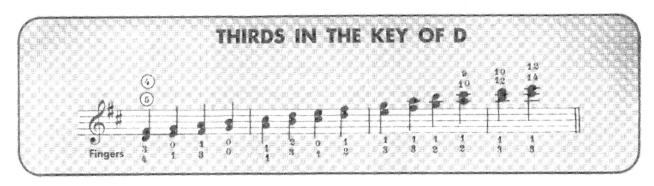

Serenade

R. de VISEE

ANDANTE IN D MAJOR

J. KÜFFNER

Sor's Etude In D Major

Moderato

Signs Appertaining To Expression and Phrasing

The Staccato: (𝅘𝅥 𝅘𝅥 𝅘𝅥 or 𝅘𝅥 𝅘𝅥 𝅘𝅥) indicate Staccato. Tones designated in this manner will be played in a disconnected style with emphasis.

𝅘𝅥 𝅘𝅥 𝅘𝅥 𝅘𝅥 : Short lines over note indicate emphasis and individuality.

𝅘𝅥 𝅘𝅥 𝅘𝅥 : Every tone marked this way should be emphasized individually and slightly separated.

> : Accent with sudden force.

Legato (⌒): All tones will be connected and played in a flowing style.

◁ : Gradual increase of intensity or volume.

▷ : Gradual diminishing of intensity.

The Swell (◁▷): Increase and diminish volume.

Gavotte

J. S. BACH
Arr. Mel Bay

Allegro Moderato

The Key of B Minor
(Relative to D Major)
THE B MINOR SCALES

Etude in B Minor

Bourree
(IN B MINOR)

JOHANN KRIEGER
1651-1735

THE CHORDS IN THE KEY OF B MINOR

The chords in the key of B Minor are Bm, Em, and F#7.

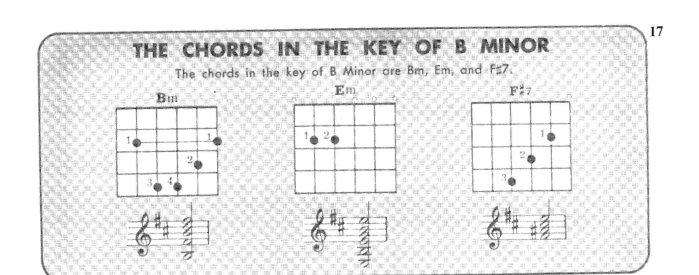

Accompaniment Styles

Love Song

Prelude in B Minor

Allegretto

SOR

GRACE NOTES

Grace notes are small-sized notes, which subtract their value from the note they precede.

The technical term for the grace note is Appoggiatura.

The grace note will be crossed at the end and will be played the same as slurs.

When the grace note is on a different string from the principal note, pick them separately.

EXAMPLES 1 and 2

The Trill

When a note alternates according to its value, very rapidly with a tone or half-tone above it the effect produced is termed the trill.

The best produced by picking the first or principal note and slurring the upper auxiliary note.

The Mordente

The Mordente is a fragment of a Trill. It is indicated by the sign: ⌁

MORE SIGNS

Tenuto (∧): Hold the tone its full value.

Rubato: Stolen from one tone and added to a tone preceding.

Luft Pause (⫽): An exaggerated pause. Uusally follows a note that is held by a hold sign, (fermata). Example: 𝄐 ⫽

The Comma (⌇) is used sometimes to indicate an interruption in the flow of tone.

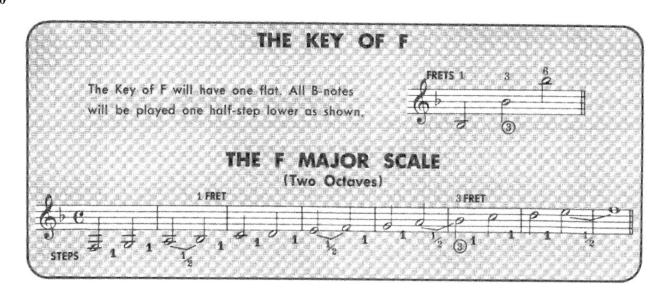

THE KEY OF F

The Key of F will have one flat. All B-notes will be played one half-step lower as shown.

THE F MAJOR SCALE
(Two Octaves)

A Daily Study

March Majestic

Arr. by Mel Bay

GUITAR SOLO

Moderato

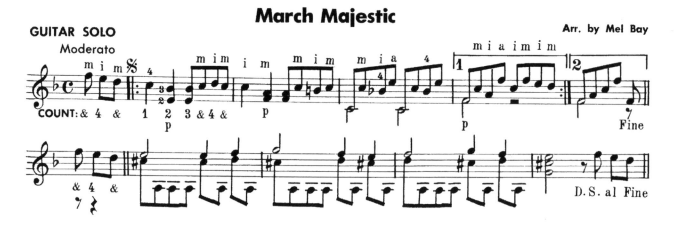

D. S. al Fine

D. S. al Fine (Dal Segno al Fine) Go back to the sign 𝄋 and play to **Fine** (the end).

Triplet Etude

In the following triplet etude employ the following Right Hand patterns: imi, mim, mam, ama.

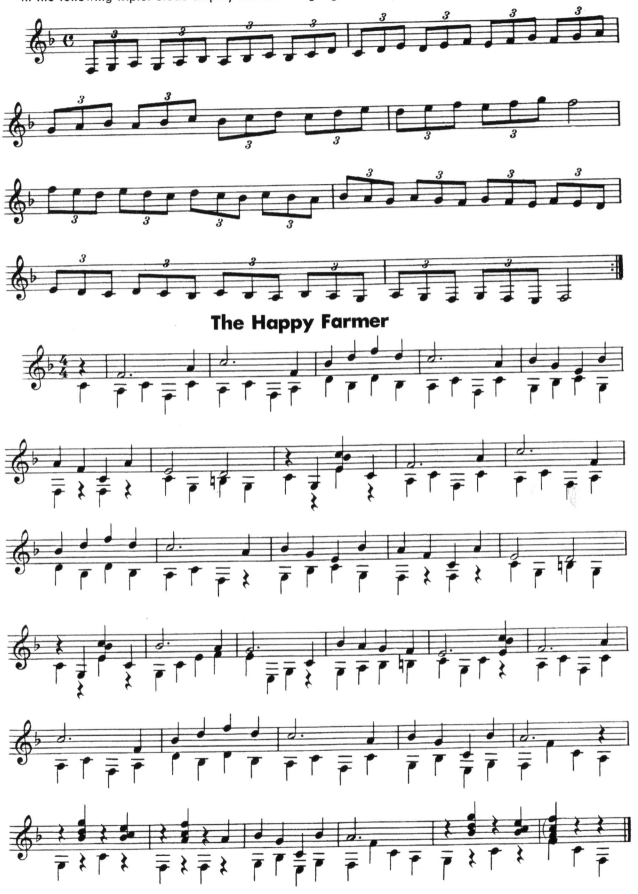

The Happy Farmer

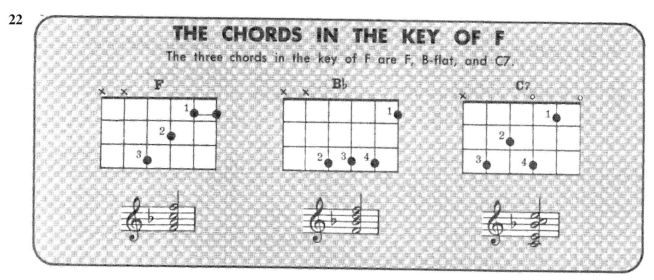

THE CHORDS IN THE KEY OF F

The three chords in the key of F are F, B-flat, and C7.

Accompaniment Styles

Common Time

Three-Four Time

Two-Four Time

Melody in F

GUITAR SOLO
Moderato

RUBENSTEIN-BAY

Minuet from Don Juan

MOZART

The Music Box

ANDANTE

F. CARULLI

THE KEY OF D MINOR
(Relative to F Major)
The D Minor Scales

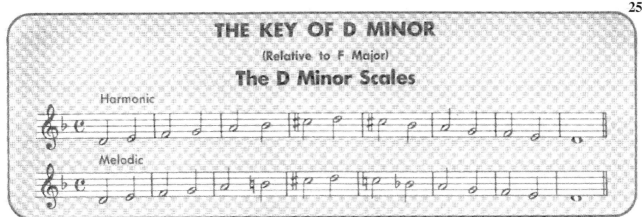

Etude in D Minor

March Slav

TCHAIKOVSKY

THE CHORDS IN THE KEY OF D MINOR

The three principal chords in the key of D minor are:

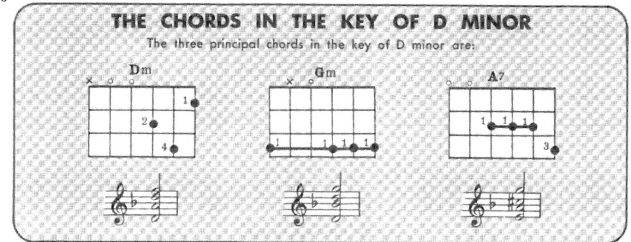

Accompaniment Styles

Common Time

Three-Four Time

Two-Four Time

Balkan Skies

GIULIANI

Andantino

Caprice

CARCASSI

THE KEY OF A

The key of A will have three sharps. (F#, C#, and G#.)

It will be identified by this signature:

The notes affected by the above signature will be played as shown:

THE A SCALE

Daily Drill

Taranto

Allegretto   CARCASSI

THE CHORDS IN THE KEY OF A

The three principal chords in the key of A are A, D, and E7

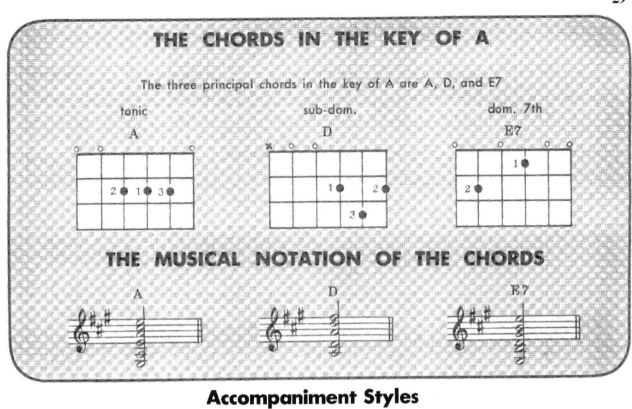

THE MUSICAL NOTATION OF THE CHORDS

Accompaniment Styles

Prelude

See the "MEL BAY FOLIO OF CLASSIC GUITAR SOLOS"

The Speedway

Fast

GUITAR SOLO
Allegretto

The Happy Guitarist

Maria

GUITAR SOLO

Arr. by Mel Bay

Andante

ANTON DIABELLI

See "MEL BAY'S DELUXE ALBUM OF CLASSIC GUITAR MUSIC"

THE KEY OF F♯ Minor
(Relative to A Major)
Two F♯ Minor Scales

Exercise

The Chords in the Key of F♯ Minor

The chords in the Key of F♯ Minor are F♯m, Bm, and C♯7.

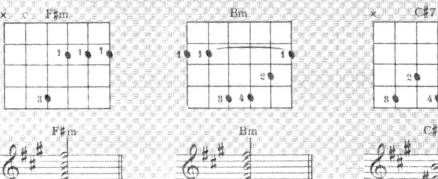

⊗ — DEADENED STRING — Kill the sound of the string with the unused part of the left hand. (See the MEL BAY CHORD SYSTEM for further explanation).

Accompaniment Styles

See "MEL BAY'S DELUXE ALBUM OF CLASSIC GUITAR MUSIC"

MORE CHROMATIC SIGNS

Up to this point we have studied and used the Sharp (#), the Flat (♭), and the Natural (♮). The student is familiar by now with their function. We now introduce the Double-Sharp and the Double-Flat.

x = Double-Sharp. A Double-Sharp will raise the sound of a tone **two frets.**

♭♭ = Double Flat. A Double-Flat will lower the sound of a tone **two frets.**

A natural will cancel all sharps, flats, double-sharps and double-flats. If a note has been double-sharped or double flatted, the return to one sharp or flat will require a natural sign followed by the desired sharp or flat.

Example:

Major To Relative Minor Etude

SIX-EIGHT TIME

This sign 𝄞 **6/8** indicates six-eight time.

6 — beats per measure
8 — type of note receiving one beat

An Eighth-note ♪ — one beat, a quarter-note ♩ — two beats and a dotted quarter note ♩. — three beats, a sixteenth-note ♬ = ½ beat.

Six-eight time consists of two units containing three beats each.

It will be counted: ♪♪♪ ♪♪♪ with the accents on beats one and four.
1 - 2 - 3 - 4 - 5 - 6

Don Quixote

AGUADO

THE DOTTED EIGHTH NOTE

A Dotted Eighth-note is equal to

EXAMPLE:

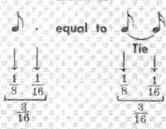

The Little Elf

Adventure

THE NOTES ON THE THIRD STRING

The notes on the third (G) string are located as shown:

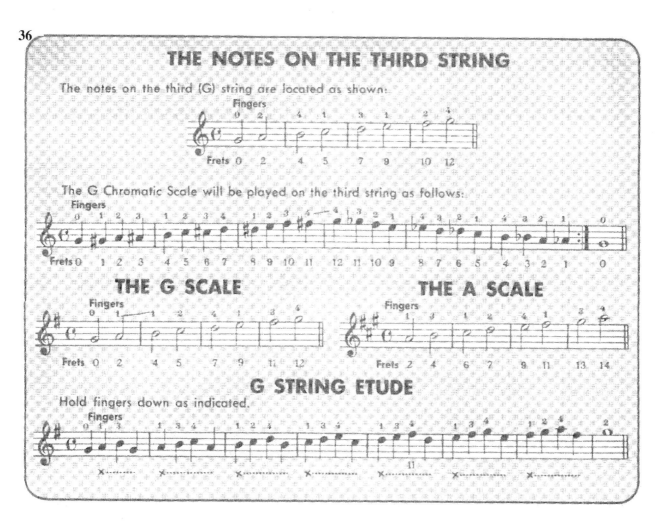

The G Chromatic Scale will be played on the third string as follows:

THE G SCALE

THE A SCALE

G STRING ETUDE

Hold fingers down as indicated.

Venetian Nights

GUITAR SOLO
Moderato

M. CARCASSI
Arr. by MEL BAY

See "MEL BAY'S DELUXE ALBUM OF CLASSIC GUITAR MUSIC"

Prelude in A Major

Andante

SOR

THE NOTES OF THE FOURTH STRING

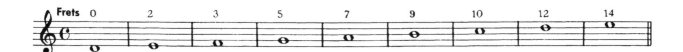

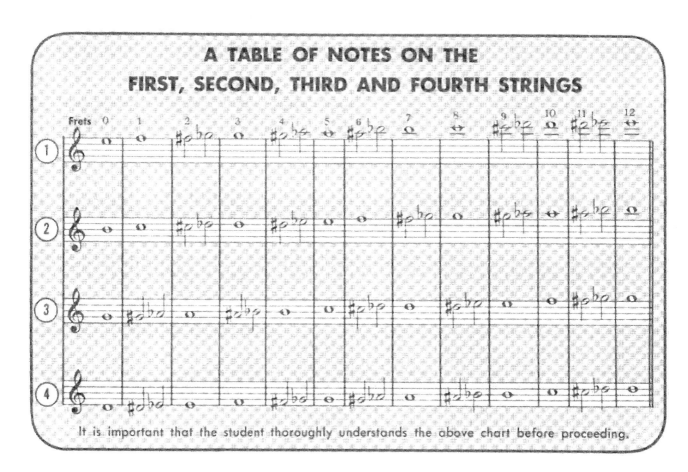

It is important that the student thoroughly understands the above chart before proceeding.

The Lido

GIULIANI

Recreation

M. GIULIANI

The Key of E Major

The key of E will have four sharps. All F, C, G, and D notes will be sharped.

THE E MAJOR SCALE

(three octaves)

Etude

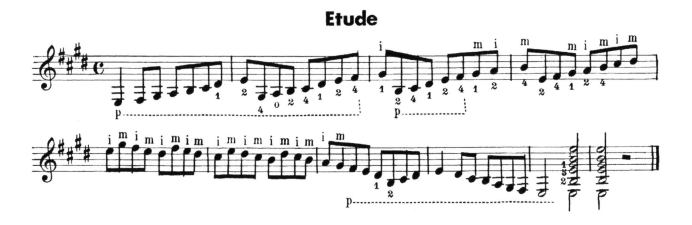

Triplet Etude in E Major

MEL BAY

THE CHORDS IN THE KEY OF E MAJOR

THE CHORDS IN THE KEY OF E MAJOR ARE: E, A AND B7.

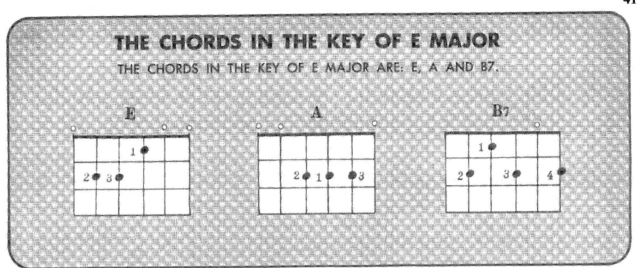

Accompaniment Styles

Prelude

See "MEL BAY'S DELUXE ALBUM OF CLASSIC GUITAR MUSIC"

Waltz in E

CARULLI

Da Capo al Fine

Frolic

SOR

Allegro

Rondo in E Major

Allegretto

Spanish Waltz

44

Soliloquy

Allegretto

See "MEL BAY'S DELUXE ALBUM OF CLASSIC GUITAR MUSIC"

Soliloquy (Cont.)

Step Lively

D.C. al Fine

ANDANTE

MOZART

Prelude

Bohemian Waltz

MEL BAY

✗ = Double sharp (see page 33)

F Double
Sharp

HARMONICS

Harmonics are produced by placing the finger of the left hand directly over certain frets pressing very lightly stopping the open string vibrations.

They are produced at the 12th, 7th, 4th and 3rd frets.

Barely touch the strings at any of the above frets quickly removing the finger as soon as the string has been struck. (Teacher should demonstrate)

Harmonics will be designated by the abbreviations: Har. 12, Har. 7, Har. 5, and Har. 4 placed over or under the note to be treated in this manner.

Harmonics are written an octave lower than they sound.

Table of Harmonics

Exercise

48

Chime Bells

(A Study in Harmonics)

Artificial Harmonics

Artifical Harmonics will enable the guitarist to play all notes on the guitar harmonically. They are performed in the following manner.

1. Place the finger of the left hand on the note desired.

2. Place the index finger of the right hand lightly on the string of desired note 12 FRETS ABOVE NOTE TO BE PLAYED.

3. Pluck the string quickly with the Right Hand Thumb stopping the tone with the pointed index finger.

Example

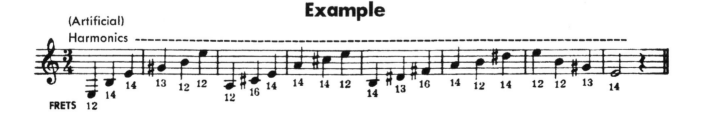

PROCEED TO "THE NEW MEL BAY CLASSIC GUITAR METHOD III"

Made in the USA
Middletown, DE
18 April 2018